INSIDE AIN'T OUT

Teresa (Resa) Farnell

authorHOUSE®

AuthorHouse™
1663 Liberty Drive
Bloomington, IN 47403
www.authorhouse.com
Phone: 1 (800) 839-8640

Published by AuthorHouse 11/16/2017

ISBN: 978-1-5462-1674-2 (sc)
ISBN: 978-1-5462-1673-5 (e)

Contents

Dedication

To all the women of the world who have sacrificed their self-image to be accepted in the eyes of mankind...not knowing that acceptance must first start within and work itself out.

Also...
My Beautiful Grandchildren
Jamie Lee II
Casey
Aleah
Rachel
Emily

Overview

Is it possible I could be fooling myself about true beauty? Is it in the eyes of the beholder or is it in the eyes of the creator? How do I begin to understand the concept of beauty until I meet the author which is the creator? Since I have been writing books, I realized you really don't know why certain items were written in a book until you have had a definite empowerment from the author's concept. Many women today think beauty is self-made and not created. Through counseling many women, I have come to the consensus; the self-made part is left up to us on what we accept. A self-image is the reflection of our thinking, whether it is optimistic or pessimistic. Many of the afflictions of women come from negative self-image. We sometimes think many of them are low social economical wives, single moms, and abuse victims, because of the negative hand which was dealt to them. You would be very surprise to know that low self-esteem has no status toward its victims. Low social economics is just a fraction of the reason women think low of themselves. Most of them don't know who they are or their sense of value. Sometimes their present situation overshadows any good they could possibility see. Women are a masterpiece, the final masterpiece from the master sculptor *"God";* this makes us a valuable commodity. It is impossible for any living creature on this earth to critique the Master of all master's art work.

How did we allow the world's views to define us? Not thin enough! Too skinny! Too fat! Too Dark! Too Light! Too old! Too young! Feel Rejected! Feeling alone! Too…Too…too…!!!!!! If we are not on this end of the spectrum we are on the other end with destructive pride. The aroma of destructive pride is not sweet at all. No one finds arrogance an attractive trait; therefore, you become rejected if you think too highly of yourself. Furthermore, you become the center of gossip or isolated because no one wants to deal with you. Your thinking becomes "high on a horse", looking down and no one else can reach you. Then you began to precede overbearing superiority over others. Therefore, began to feel empty and have only your thoughts to befriend. Suddenly you become your worst enemy. The persecutor and the persecuted paint a pretty picture of your character. Where is the balance? If you think low of yourself no one wants you, and if you think highly of yourself no one wants you. Either way, both prove that the world has conditions that you must meet.

What happened to unconditional love? Now you find yourself hitting the gym, dealing with eating disorders, dealing with depression, spending beyond your means, painful cosmetic surgery, tolerating abusive relationships, or abusing yourself; all due to the lack of a healthy positive self-concept of who you are. The list goes on and on, but the point of this book is not to glorify how the world took over. On the contrary, this book will make you aware of the traps set before you. In each chapter, you will see biblical insight as well as a woman's personal reflections. Also, the reader will be able to engage their past perspective and reflect on future insight.

"Inside Ain't Out" will navigate you through a mirror to reveal the half-truths you have been fed. The reflection the world gives you is only one sided and there are so many beautiful attributes you are neglecting. However, to discover them you should turn to your heart inside and compass it toward the Master's word. Through the pages of this book you will discover how your inner beauty outlines your appearance. We will unmask the fragile and impressionable woman and restore the confidence in which you are heir through a heavenly kingdom. Through the authority given to you in scripture; you will discover how to eradicate the negativity and allow positive qualities to take root, nurture and develop.

God's word is designed to refocus you from what the world thinks of you, to what He thinks of you. In doing this, you will keep your human responsibility and protect yourself from destruction. Through the grace of God, you will regenerate your mind to reveal the image the world has hid. Finally, you will discover how to achieve a balance and know self- worth and reaffirm your value. Now when the final page is flipped you will get a glimpse of God's affection and yet find it totally invigorating, and it's only a glimpse! Once you know who you are; it will be difficult to see yourself any other way. Only a heart after God's heart leaves a legacy. I pray this book will effectively rebuild you into a positive individual through the power of the one true love, God the Father, The Son and The Holy Ghost.

Introduction

The masterpieces of God were finalized when He made woman. Ever since then, women have captivated grace and beauty. You must see yourself through the eyes of the master sculptor "God". You are a spirit being in an earthly body. You were not only created, but sculptured from the hands of God and the image of Christ; this makes you unique and distinguishes you from anyone else. Every part of your body illuminates the permanent self-image that God has given you. When God created woman, he was finish with his workmanship of creating mankind. Therefore, this gives you evidence man was not complete until the woman was created. There was evidence in the eyes of the Father, He wanted to complete the beauty of mankind through woman. Notice, women started the battle in the beginning and we will probably end the battle in the end. Nevertheless, women were created to balance the universe. Therefore, we as women must get ourselves together and get back to claiming our worth without having tangible items attach to us to identify our value. We are valuable when we are naked. Eve was valuable naked. God has placed in every living creature the ability to have self-awareness. Self-awareness comes with no attachments on with innermost parts…come as you are. The personality of a person has been shaped and conformed before they were even born. Many characteristics attack your soul, because you don't know who you are. Many have defined self-esteem as feelings of worth based on their accomplishments, status, financial resources, or appearance. This kind of self-esteem leads a person to feel independent, prideful, and indulge in self-worship, which diminishes your desire to please God.

Most of the time when we are hurting or dealing with some type of pain, we tend to be draw toward a negative energy and pride is one of them. But for the victim of the circumstance it seems like the perfect place to land, it seems safe. Pride is a cover up for one's true self-image. I am not talking about the pride which we all should have; the pride of keeping ourselves feeling good about ourselves and not putting others down with it. I am discussing the pride which looks tall and forgets others are beneath them and tramples overs those which someday might just become their boss one day. It can cause you to steal the identity of someone else. By doing this, you become unaware of your personal attributes God has created just for you. Therefore, you began to move toward coveting unhealthy pride because you really don't know your identity. I call it unhealthy pride because it drives you away from God's moral excellence and integrity. You become more concern about what others think. This type of pride is a signal of not knowing who you are, so you try to fit into someone else's mold. This is one of the reasons pride gives off such a drastic odor in the nostrils of God. When something has an odor, it keeps others a distance from it. In other words, even if you were in a valuable position no one could see you because no one would dare come close. Everyone should have some type of pride in their life, but the pride we should have is the one that is so soft that to the touch that we can feel it, man can sense it and God is the only one who can understand it. I believe this is when society began to pull God's kingdom definitions. To know the genuine definition of self-worth is in the kingdom of God (*only the creator knows the genuine definition, we just practice, we haven't got it right yet!*) …people on the other hand began to say they are tooting their own horn, or know it all's…but in turn, they are just dealing out what was given to them before they were born. The hand can't keep all this information in too long, *in other words*, the task master gave this knowledge to you for a reason.

Mind thing…

When your spirit man is renewed; then your mind begins to transform into your identity, but you must allow the spirit to dictate to your mind. Stop blocking the spirit from molding you into the beautiful person you were ordained to be! On a biblical perspective; God is responsible for the positive attributes you possess. This enables you to even attempt to build your self-esteem. Self-esteem from a biblical standpoint is not built, but revealed through you, because God has already formed it into your character from the beginning. God is good and good is positive. God recognized the positive self-esteem in women long before you were even thought of.

In the old testament, the women were proud and walk with their heads up high and had seductive eyes. These characteristics where of women who thought their outer appearance was more important. It also, causes them to lose out on receiving the true wisdom of beauty. When you consider the mirror ask yourself, is it real or fake? Only God knows the real deal. God put a lot of emphasis on the inward man because this is who you are. If we spend countless times on the outside, why not spend countless time on the inside. Ask yourself who is more valuable?

In "Inside Ain't Out" I will share with you my past perspectives and divine understanding. I realized that it was the inside who allowed myself to become the person I was, am, and about to be. Change always starts with your thoughts. A person must realize that before you were even form in the belly of your mother, it wasn't about "me"; it was about God's will and purpose being fulfilled in your life. "Inside-Out" gives a detail image of who, what, and why we were born. The focus is not "me" but "Him" (God our father) the creator. Every single moment of your life has been carefully crafted and shaped to fit the mold that God has created just for His glory. This book will assist women all over the world to accept their surrounding beauty, body image and build healthy self-concept, knowing before you were formed in the wound of your mother, you are wonderfully and beautifully made. Through "Inside Ain't Out" you will realize true beauty comes from the inside and flows outside. There is a condition behind this beauty; it only happens when you accept God's view of beauty. Remember: you are called for "HIS "purpose. Positive mind is not transform through status but through state of mind. Remember: the imperfections in us reveal the perfection in God.

Chapter 1

Beautifully Sculptured

God predestined the creation of man and woman before the foundation of the earth, but He prepares the earth before bringing them into existence. Therefore, God stated "It is not good for man to be along." God always does things at the right time. The episodes of allowing earth and man to become established first before bringing in the woman, was the all-wise plan for mankind. God prepared the man and earth for the astonishing announcement of woman. He had big plans for a woman. This was just the genesis of women becoming the ultimate beauty of life. Through this one woman "Eve" God laid the platform and mold for the transition of beauty and love. Without woman, man could not express person to person humanistic love and could not respond to the intimacy of another human being. Man's ambitions didn't begin to arise until another human being came in the picture to arouse the play. Therefore, God had to give man someone to keep him on his toes which of course you know it was... woman.

BUILT BY THE MASTER'S HAND...

A good artist sculpts his masterpiece to perfection. Sometimes the piece may fight the sculptor, but once the sculpture is complete, it is inspected for any scratchers or imperfections. It is up to the clay to remain in position, so the artist can properly mold and shape it into what the masterpiece will be. It becomes the artist masterpiece even before it is presented to the public, because the sculptor has felt the sensation in his hands which beholds the perfection. His eyes are radiant as he adds a piece of clay piece by piece. The more he feels the sensation the more the complete picture of perfection comes into play. It was through him feeling the needs of each piece determined the complete and final perfect creation which births a renowned masterpiece. Any other word, God is the sculptor and you are the masterpiece.

Since you are his craftsmanship, let's talk about the first masterpiece, which is always the pathway for others.

The woman for Adam was made from existing elements like Adam's creation. The existing elements came from Adam – namely his ribs.

²¹ And the LORD God caused a deep sleep to fall upon Adam, and he slept: and he took one of his ribs, and closed the flesh instead thereof;

²² And the rib, which the LORD God had taken from man, made he a woman, and brought her unto the man (Genesis 2:21-22) KJV

God, "The Great Physician" performed surgery on Adam by using his DNA (first DNA performance) flesh of my flesh bone of my bone. God also put him to sleep (first anesthesiologist surgery), and removed a rib. The existing elements in woman came from Adam. This meant the same DNA, cell structure, and blood type. Biologically woman is the same as man. God boost us up a little, so we can be attracted to the opposite sex. Woman had so many distinguish characteristic until Adam couldn't help but say "woo-man".

From the rib, the Lord "made" the woman. The word *made* means *built*. The Hebrew word, *"built" is "banah"* which means to build, to construct. Therefore, this means the woman was *"built"*. She was a beautiful creature, built from Adam for Adam. Adam had simply been sculptured *(Hebrew, "jatsar")* from clay; but the woman was built. When something is built, there must be a blue print, therefore God, use the sculpture of Adam to identify the completion of man, woman. The architecture, symmetry, and beauty were the crowning glory of all creation.

Woman was created from the rib of a man, the part of a man that guards the heart and other vital organs in the lower respiratory system. You can ask yourself, Why God only took the ribs from the man and then closed the flesh without taking any other organs of the body? The rib protects the vital organs of the body. The ribs are a cage around the heart, therefore when God took a rib from the man; he took part of the protection of the heart, which in turn made his guard of the heart incomplete (open for something). The pathway was opened for God to complete man by creating a counterpart, woman. Considering the strength and protection of the bodies' vital organs, God took one of the ribs of man to create woman. Man's rib guarding the heart of woman …sounds good to me! God was giving you a part of strength and protection from man.

WOMAN DISTINCTIVE PARTS…

God created some distinctive parts just for the woman. One of them is her reproductive organs. These organs were created inside of her to prepare her for what was to come, "Be fruitful and multiply" and for the barren woman, trust God the creator to demonstrate a miracle beyond her imperfection (whether she bares a child or not).

"Unto the woman he said, I will greatly multiply thy sorrow and they conception; in sorrow thou shalt bring forth children;" (Genesis 3:16) KJV

You were placed into this world to help man tend to the beauty and creations of God. The most important person you were created to glorify is God. Not just with your mouth but also with your body. How can we be beautifully sculptured? By the Glory of God, He has placed in us from the beginning of time. Beauty comes from the inside of the body and penetrates to the surface of the other body parts. It does not come from the outside; it comes from the inside and nurtures the body on the outside to Glorify God. The same way positivity and negativity births on the inside and moves to the outward. *"Beautifully made"* starts in our thought patterns. Any time you see beautiful people in spirit there must have been a spiritual battle on the inside. You choose who dominates your kingdom! You are negative because you choose to be negative. You are positive because you choose to be positive. Whatever the outcome is, the final home plate is up to who you allow to win in your mind. The *world's* concept of beautiful *means* your outer appearance, your clothes, hair, etc.

Don't get me wrong, it's okay to adorn your body with pretty things, but don't let this define your beauty. Have you ever redecorated your house and no matter what you put in it, it still doesn't look right? Well.. sometimes it is not the furniture that makes it beautiful. Most of the time it is where you put the furniture and how you present it to the viewer, because every clue or definite thought comes from how the individual views the situation. Therefore, a positive mind is very important and vital to the standards of true beauty. Godly beauty starts with the way you think; your mind penetrates thoughts which act out into your outward appearance:

22 That ye put off concerning the former conversation the old man, which is corrupt according to the deceitful lusts;

23 And be renewed in the spirit of your mind;

24 And that ye put on the new man, which after God is created in righteousness and true holiness. (Ephesians 4: 22-24, KJV)

God specifically commanded us to be renewed in the spirit of our mind. This renewing is very vital toward growing into the grace and beauty God has prepared for you. Your spiritual person is the one who should dictate your character, but because we have gotten the wrong concept of beauty, we tend to allow our eyes to do the talking. Therefore, everything we see becomes our compass for beauty. If you allow the spirit of God to cultivate your thought patterns beauty will differentiate individuals. Since this is the case, you must renew the thought of being beautiful from the carnal thinking to the spiritual thinking. Beauty in the spiritual sense is always putting God as the goal of your purpose and relying on these words, "I am already beautiful…I am unique, and no one is like me and never will be". True beauty does not pronounce itself outwardly, but it allows the beholder to create its own picture. Therefore, beauty is in the eyes of the beholder. The things you might not see, the beholder does. Beauty is a word that only the Creator and the beholder can explain.

30 Favour is deceitful, and beauty is vain: but a woman that feareth the LORD, she shall be praised." (Proverbs 31:30) KJV

Woman was created to glorify the beauty of God. He is graceful, and He is wonderful. These traits seem to stick with women forever. Therefore, to glorify God we must fear the Lord and remain in His order, especially on the definition of beauty. In fearing God, we are showing him we appreciate the beauty He bestowed upon us as being a woman. Just because, you are not recognized by man as being the most beautiful woman, doesn't mean you are not beautiful. Beauty considers the action in the eyes of God, rather than a physical attraction of man.

When God performed the first operation He constructed every single detail to perfection which shows her femininity. He even put the desire into woman to have a sense of belonging. When God brought her to man, I believe the way retrospectively women were design, man knew she was a special glorification created by God just for him. A woman is different and unique from man, when it comes to character and spirit. A woman is the balance for man. She tends to have more of an emotional part of her which can feel the intimacy and heart of others. Women tend to balance the world, because they see more than black and white when it comes to situations. The situation could be green, but because of her faith and creativity, she sees what she believes. Therefore, her outer appearance has always been a battle because she was given certain features that attract the opposite sex. Since then, women have built their self-image, self-esteem, and self- awareness on the way they appear to others.

Chapter 2

Inside Out Beauty

So…the woman in the mirror keeps harassing you! She keeps telling you negative things about the way you look. Why are you allowing yourself to become vulnerable to her? The more you consider the mirror the more she controls you. This is unhealthy! It can either make you! Drive you! Or destroy you! This person in the mirror will drive you into thinking self-perfection is real and lead you to self-destruction. Who is this woman? Haven't you figured it out? Of course, it's you! The person in mirror has become your personal enemy. Since that first glance, you have been looking for ways toward perfection. Whether you recognize it or not this type of thinking is unhealthy. Unhealthy self-awareness can encounter so much control until you won't be able to see the real deal- "you". You began to view perfection on how others see you. The media and Hollywood has given you the false meaning of beauty. All we have to do is put it on a billion-dollar baby and it gets the approval of the media and now it makes million's off ordinary people like us. It is so strange how a regular sister can wear it and she can be call ghetto and put it on a sister in Hollywood and now everybody is wearing it and not just that, it is now making millions on the stock market. This is a Lie! Straight from Hell!

Who is now dictating our value? Earth or heaven? God values the inner beauty of a gentle and quiet spirit over physical attractiveness. When you become attentive, you tend to listen more and talk less. You notice the traps the devil has set up to place our pocketbooks up to spend more and value less. As a woman, you can be so critical of yourself until you miss out on the real purpose of life. You can end up spending your entire life looking at your hair, face, body, clothing etc. This list can go on and on if you keep looking. Each time you scope out one thing not right on your body or etc., you discover something else on the other hand need tweeting. The parts you keep trying to tweet becomes filled with emptiness, because the more you mold and shape the more you keep finding another thing to tweet... it's a never-ending cycle. In other words, it is not who you are, it is what you are! The outer appearance is only a cover to what's going on inside. It doesn't reflect the real "you". Therefore, your perfection becomes a mirror image and not reality. Before you know it, you will be a just mannequin everybody looking at and wondering what new adventure you are going to bring out next. In other words, "existing and not living". Before long you will start hearing whispering voices in the atmosphere saying things like this, *"Every time I see her she has something new done to her body"* or, *"What she done did now"* and the list can go on. These are signals pointing to some main directions.

The scripture quotes in I Peter 3: 3-4 (KJV) states "Whose adorning let it not be that outward adorning of plaiting the hair, and of wearing of gold, or of putting on of apparel;

4 But let it be the hidden man of the heart, in that which is not corruptible, even the ornament of a meek and quiet spirit, which is in the sight of God of great price."

In other words, beauty can become corruptible by the adornment of a woman, especially when you build your image on it. Everything you do to try to make yourself perfect becomes vanity, because it becomes a continuous cycle with a never-ending purpose. We are Kingdom Princesses and our beauty goes beyond our adornment! People turn their heads because they see the spirit of kingdom daughters beyond looks. The admiration of love, grace and mercy are the spiritual aroma that is placed upon the kingdom princess lives. Beauty is in the eyes of the beholder and God is the controller of beauty anyhow, therefore let's rely on him to define it.

Let's look at how man's definition of beauty is vastly taking on society today. To gain perfect body shape of 32-22- 32, women workout at the gym daily, deprive themselves of delicious high calorie foods, just to end up a few months later hating the results. Cosmetic and plastic surgeons are getting richer by the minute on the fictional definition of beauty and those who can't afford it, do what they can to gain it. But where did this come from? Is society getting to the point…self-image is all about how you look? Where is positive personality? Where is perfection? Does it mean the outer appearance? Society has gotten a misconception of what beauty is. An overindulge appearance can cause you to be driven into a world of deceit. For instance, purchasing an expensive $100,000 car when your finances can only afford a $20,000 one or buying a $50,000 handbag but when you look inside you only have $5 to put inside of it. Entertaining these kinds of concepts is unhealthy, excessive and causes you to walk into a dangerous level of pride. It's okay to be overly confident in you and what you do and to value yourself, but when you allow the things you possess, the people who possess them, to control you to keep the status rolling, you are walking on thin ice and causing the norm of pride to rise beyond glass ceiling. What is the world dictating to us! Simply deceptive, overextended high driven pride! But at the End of the day, where is you? Are you happy? Are you Satisfied with your life?

Driven by the concept of beauty and fame…

Don't misinterpret what I am saying. Don't get me wrong, you should take care of your body and feel good about yourself, because it is the place the Holy Spirit resides. The temple is the shell, but don't let your temple live with only you in mind. You must not forget, you are not the only one at home, hello! You are not alone in this body! Think about it.

Think about it…when you take in a roommate in your house, the both of you still should come to a consensus on major changes in the household. How would you like to pay rent or a mortgage and never make any decisions on where you live? Jesus paid the redemption price for our sins and opened the door for the Holy Ghost to live inside of us and we don't even recognize Him when it comes to our body.

BEAUTY REST

Beauty that rests inside gives you a permanent fixture…it never moves! With this type of beauty, you know longer see yourself from the outside.

Therefore, a bad hair day becomes just what it is, *"a bad hair day"* not *"a bad hair for life"*. Every part of you flows from within, especially when your spiritual mind becomes alive. Whether you know it are not, when a person began to see themselves the way they are; true beauty can give off a radiant of light. *Behold!* The beauty is magnified through the beholder. Now the way you feel becomes your personality, because you are reflecting our Heavenly Father. You become a real person and not an actor. All the other stuff you do to make yourself feel good becomes just perks toward your character.

Remember, God is the one who gives you the foundation of your personality. Before you were born, He had already decided what to equip your mind with, so you could perform your purpose on this earth. You may only see a fracture of the equipment now, but keep living you will see some things come out of you which will zap you for a moment. But it is you! This is the phrases of your personality being exposed at the right time. Therefore, it is our responsibility to stay connected, because God's responsibility has already been placed inside of you. Our job is to cultivate and protect what God has already given us. It is up to the Master Sculptor God, to decide what the finish product should look like, but it is also up to you to allow the sculptor to finish the product. Therefore, stop jumping off the Wheel!

"9 Woe unto him that striveth with his Maker! Let the potsherd strive with the potsherds of the earth. Shall the clay say to him that fashioneth it, What makest thou? or thy work, He hath no hands?" (Isaiah 45: 9 NIV)

Complaining about the way you look is an insult to the Master Sculptor. It's as though women are telling God the way He created you was all wrong! To reject God's foundation is to reject His creative ability. I found myself critiquing the Master sculpture's masterpiece and realize that I was not qualified to even given it a test. The problem is not the sculptor, but the clay. We tend to jump in an out of God's hand and then blame it on Him for the outcome. God is a free will God. If you don't desire to become that beautiful piece he has already predestined, this is your chose, but please don't blame God.

Driven by Self...

Taking a quick look at yourself is the best way to keep yourself positive about whom you are. If you look to long, you began to see more than you need to see. Self-image has driven a lot of women to the point of disappointment and low self- esteem, because society has dictated to you the way you look portrays the way you feel; not necessary so. The word "self-esteem" has become a misleader for lots of women in the world today. Some say, "If you think highly of yourself ...you have a high self-esteem". This statement creates a false image which has dominates the minds of women for years. For one to think highly, your inner spirit is in denial, which allows you to explode into deceit, hurt and pain. I can remember in one of the workshops I was facilitating, I ask the women to fill out a self-evaluation of the feelings they had about themselves. There was one woman who was smiling and said, "I know I am going to pass this test because I love myself". By the time, I finish the workshop this woman was in tears, she stated, "I thought because I dressed up and look good, I had it together...but by being in this class I realized it take more than a "look" to feel good about yourself." This woman had a lot of hidden hurt inside of her. Close friends had broken her heart; therefore, she covered it up by making herself the project. She constantly spent money on things she thought would make her happy. There was still a void in her life. She realized first, she had to forgive herself for allowing her friends to control her life. Second, she had to forgive the friends and let it go. You can't change people, but you can change the way you think about them. After this moment, her eyes were open to the true person inside of her. The hurt was driving her to please others instead of herself. Until you recognize the deceit you are hiding behind, you will never be able to see the real person in the mirror.

Positive self-esteem is a process that has many domains to considered, but arrives at the same consensus, "feeling good about you inside and out". One way many women feel good about themselves are to "esteem themselves". Sometimes this can cause you to be a hypocrite "thinking more than whom you are", especially when you put others down when they are less fortunate than you. By doing this, you do not nurture the humility in spiritual growth God is calling for. You are valuable, and you should value yourself, but please don't value yourself at the cost of your brother or sister.

Better yet, you are a diamond, but sometimes women are "diamond in the dirt" ...other words, been covered up so long, till you don't see the real worth.

"Get out the dirt Girl!"

Beauty longing not lasting...

There is a place God desire woman to move forward into. This place is where your inner beauty outshines the outer beauty. This is the place where you have established a value, and no one can put a price tag on you...not even you. God wants you to get to the place of not needing to esteem yourself, but enjoy the benefits of having an intensive relationship flowing through you and radiating outwardly. Women should get to the point where they are not self-directed for attention. You should have such a love for God until your image and self-esteem is based on the foundation of God. But this isn't and overnight trip. This level of esteem comes through spending countless times in the word, praying and building a personal relationship with God. When He becomes your friend, He will then become your role model. By doing the above mention things you are allowing God to be the judge and the juror of your perfection.

Everything that women fight for has already been won through the word. Women are trying to fight esteem with carnal weapons. Don't you know we have already won? The problem is you are in the ring fighting when you should be outside the ring being a cheerleader. Everything you are fighting to be have already been conqueror. Quit using your energy fighting something you already won! You do a lot of overtime spending money for tangible beauty. Every time you buy one product, another product comes out promoting it can do the job better. It's not just beauty products, but weight programs, society statuses, and other vanity items which esteem you as being successful. Whatever you fight with becomes the conqueror. So, if your weapons become carnal, your battle will be carnal, but if your weapons are mighty in God, then your battle will be mighty in God. Don't get me wrong, God wants you to love yourself. If you love yourself, you will seek the ultimate, beneficial good for yourself. By doing this you will be promoting beauty in the kingdom of God

Where can you find that inner beauty everyone is talking about? First, you must realize that you are not in this by yourself; God is responsible for every positive attribute you possess.

3 Know ye that the LORD he is God: it is he that hath made us, and not we ourselves; we are his people, and the sheep of his pasture. (Psalm 100:3) KJV

Since God created us he knew what attributes to place upon you for His perfect will and purpose. It is not the outside that God wants to shine, because whatever is inside will come out, sooner or later. God does not value our intelligence when it is exalted apart from Him.

God wants the inner woman to become more sensitive to His perfect will. When you become more sensitive to the inner person, the outer person becomes less dominate to control your fleshly appetite. Over indulged self-image contributes to your fleshly appetite. Self-image only portrays what you think the inner spirit is. Until you come into the true knowledge of your divine master's will and purpose, you will continue to feed and nurture the flesh. You can always tell a woman that has found her inner spirit; she has acquired a lot of wisdom, *"Self"* no longer dominates outwardly. I am not saying she is not successful, pretty or classy, but in turn her personality and character is no longer *"all about me"*. Furthermore, her inner person shines so brightly, even the fleshly flaws she encounters in the future are barely noticeable.

Chapter 3

Fragile and Impressionable

In Chapter 2 we discussed self-esteem and self-image and how the negative concepts of them can lead you into a life of being a hypocrite. Healthy self-esteem is essential to obtain happiness and appreciation for life. There are four domains to consider when dealing with self-awareness, which leads to correcting the wise tales on self-esteem and self- image.

Appearance...

The first is *"appearance" which* means the way something looks or formed. The Greek word for "appearance" is *"eidos"* which means appearance, fashion, shape or sight. When we study the definition of the word appearance we realized that the signals all point to something you see. But I believe that God was talking about another appearance which you see with the spiritual eye which is the *"heart"*.

"...⁷ But the LORD said unto Samuel, Look not on his countenance, or on the height of his stature; because I have refused him: for the LORD seeth not as man seeth; for man looketh on the outward appearance, but the LORD looketh on the heart. *(I Samuel 16:7) KJV*

God values the inner beauty over the outer attractions of a woman. He even said in His word that He honors a quiet and meek spirit. The world system has greatly camouflage beauty, emphasizing the outside attraction dominating greatly the inside attractions. Therefore, the devil deceives women, especially when it comes to her looks, character, abilities, and even decision making. I can recall in the Garden of Eden when Eve was deceived my Satan. She was told not to touch the tree of good and evil, but because of the deception of the devil, whom appeared to her in a cunning spirit, lured her into admiring the tree until it looked good for food. Because of the covenant, God had made with Adam and Eve, Eve probably never saw the tree good for food, until the incident with Satan. In Similarity, if you constantly admire something, you are bound to find something appealing, which sometimes will pull you into a world of deceit and disappointment.

Outer Appearance is only a cover for the real deal. The real deal is in the mind, because the mind shapes the heart. Whatever is in a man's heart will come out. The mind feeds the heart. The mind tells the heart what to keep and what to spit out. Our action shows what the mind has been entertaining. So, the real deal is your inner person.

In the spirit realm, appearance is the shape of the person. The word *"shape"* refers to your mind. The mind shapes you into the person you ought to be, whether it is inner or outer appearance. When the mind is being renewed, the appearance becomes renewed. Just as shaping is a process, the renewing of the mind is a process. For something to be renewed, you must first be able to realize that you have left the original state. Sometimes it is very difficult to realize that you have drifted far to the left, until it becomes a constant problem. Most of the time you don't know you have a problem with self-image, until you recognize the changes you have made is not enough; this is when your battle begins. The launch to change has plant a never-ending seed into your mind. Furthermore, you began a journey of personal improvement. The mind can cause you to see more than your eyes can understand, in which can cause trickery to your self-image. Therefore, it is important for the way you think to transform.

"And do not be conformed to this world, but be transformed by the renewing of your mind, that you may prove what is that good and acceptable and perfect will of God." (Romans 12:2 NIV)

A few years ago, I had an encounter with a female who was very; entangled with herself and life. She wanted to be that perfect woman with a perfect life. She began to desire to look a certain way, have a career, and own certain things that portrayed *"worldly status"*. She kept to herself and didn't conversant much with people. She thought being quiet meant her inner character was okay. Through counseling this person, I found out all this massive control started through her father first, then she began to have relationship with men encountering the same behavior. She didn't identify the control factor therefore, she was lead into a web of deceit for many years. Guess what? This was the beginning of her becoming the control mannequin with the perfect life looking through the eyes of someone else and there was no turning back. She was dancing with the devil and walking with God. In the beginning, it felt good because She wanted to feel accepted first and then secondly, she wanted to be loved liked everybody else. She didn't know control was not an attribute of love. She thought when someone love you they control you. All her life she saw control as a factor of acceptance, therefore she felt it was okay to be control, until it became uncontrollable. She became uncontrollable, her life became uncontrollable. Her psychological, social, mental, and physiological life became chaos.

Here come some of the results....

She was recommended to see her spiritual mentor and a psychiatrist. I believed this young lady had a purpose in life and the enemy wanted her life to be aborted. This was a strong woman. She kept fighting for the perfect life. I watch her from a far off. She kept trying to get that perfect job. She was highly educated. She was climbing successfully, and all the physical changes was pointed toward preparing for that perfect job. She desired to have a position in the world that told people that she was somebody. She ignored the signals from God; all along God was trying to capture her attention. One thing about God, if you have a purpose He will use your adversities to point you back to your purpose. I even saw God's hand put walls up in the directions she was headed, but look like she was determined to break down the walls. I could see she was tired of being controlled, but didn't know how to go about taking over the driving wheel. You must be dumb or a superwoman to think you can knock down walls in God's divine will. After doing all of this, she still couldn't recognize she had a major problem with self-esteem and self-image. More trials and tribulations happen in her life for her to recognize exactly what was really going on. God doesn't want us to base our beauty on the outward attractions, because it will soon vanish through the age of time. Through the years of trying to make yourself successful and beautiful you will realize it is just a temporary fix. The problem wasn't her image it was her mind. She needed to let go of hurt from her father, sisters and especially her spouse who had first, physically abuse her in her earlier years and later it continually stretched into mental abuse. I spoke with her recently and she finally settled the hurt of her father on his death bed 16 years ago, sadly to say. He apologized to her with tears in his eyes…. of course, it freed her of the hurt from him. A few years later after her father passed away she settle the debt of separation from her sisters in which her father kept them apart with the dangerous gossip of spreading rumors about each sister to each other. They finally realized he was the one keeping them apart and today they are reconciling their relationships more and more. Even though she was carrying around this heavy control mechanism in her life she was determine to see her true self again…

Finally, it was time to go into her war closet. She was not ready; People would ask her sometimes why she stayed in the relationship so long. She couldn't answer the question, but I do know, if you make up your mind to leave any situation, don't think, just leave, because if you think, you began to manipulate your mind with "what if" and before long you will be right back where you started. She was on antidepressants for over two decades trying to cover-up hurt and pain of a life time of abuse. Her heart just didn't want to hurt her spouse. That is funny, because on the other hand he was a good man to her. Even though, her spouse had given his life over to going to church and everything, it didn't change the hurt and pain that was living inside of her.

Quit Fake It till You Make it! There is no Such Thing!

You can't cover-up when you mess -up. You can't temporary deliver either. Many times, she wanted to walk out the door, but he was a master manipulator. He would often say some cunning words to pull her right back into his arms and make her feel like yesterday was only a dream. I can't believe she stayed so many years into this situation. I wouldn't recommend any sister, aunt, mother, cousin, daughter or friend to stay in a controlling relationship like this. She lost herself, friends, family and most of all since of control. The sad part about a controlling partner, they believe they are the victim, when you talk to them about it. It becomes wall paper on the wall; seen and not heard. I don't blame them! I blame their fathers for not showing the intimate side to their sons in the homes.

I am not talking about showing sex in front of them. I am talking about showing affection; such as, kissing your wife in front of your kids going or coming home. Special times when she is washing dishes, give her a tickle or something...show Johnny...it is not about sex in the bedroom, but about catching the ball in the kitchen and touchdown happens in the bedroom. Sometimes the children need to see daddy and mommy running around the house chasing around the chairs and laughing. If children, see formal family than they will have formal families and they will have formal marriages and the cycle will return. Love and affection needs to be shown in the families. Christians have so many divorces, because we fail to balance our lives. We can teach Jesus, but let's teach Jesus saving marriages. Somehow, we forget Jesus was God walking on earth showing us how to live as man till he returns. I believe God probably looks down on us and say, "They are trying to be God's on earth." We are supposed to be living on earth. God told Adam and Eve to be fruitful and multiply. You can't multiply by just looking at each other and you must interact to perform...I hope you got that!

Sometimes we are too busy being religious; reaching up to God, when He has already given us Jesus who came down and gave us Christianity which gives us relationship. Now we have intimacy. It is so funny how we claim we have intimacy with God, but can't have intimacy with our mates. Therefore, we cannot blame some of our spouses for their actions.

Even though I help this other woman, it was really helping me, and I could confess these words to myself,

"Due to me holding on to my relationship of abuse, my situations could never be use as a testimony for others because I felt my spouse was always controlling me with his eyes in the audience, because he wasn't free. But, this was what the ministry was about, "freeing women". My life had been through mostly 99 percent of the situations women had been through. Even though the audience was ready for the ultimate breakthrough I couldn't go into maximum overdrive because he would control the situation through his eyes. I was too busy trying to cover up his life and save him from shame. But it wasn't about my spouse, it was about my assignment from God. I knew if I told my story this would give the ultimate ice-breaker for that desperate sister looking for that special breakthrough for years.... I had to make up my mind and let go

and let God. It was draining the ministry inside of me. I couldn't do what God had call me to do, because of the pride of my spouse, the pride inside of me, and so I decided to let go and walk away. I could no longer be a hypocrite as a woman, minister, counselor, nor friend. I finally awakened. I walked away from a 34-year marriage of bondage and walked into a purpose driven life."

No more being a hypocrite…I was ready to take up my cross….

You become a slave to life instead of living life, when you try to band aid past hurt many years trying to make myself perfect, not realizing the person I long to be was hidden behind scabs of hurt. I felt and looked beautiful outside, but my inside was all messed up and distorted. I had stacks of hurt which needed to be deleted from my life. The only way I could let go the hurt; I had to first see the situation clearly. It was through God; I could see the picture clearly. I was a victim, but not for long, because God help me to see my inner person. When I saw, my inner person was longing for happiness, I decided to let her take control. You must see good in the people who hurt you and this is not easy. Through Jesus Christ Blood, I could see good, grace and mercy. Also, began to have compassion for them and prayed for them, because they also were victims. But, this doesn't mean to allow them to continue to hurt you. There comes a point in your life you should let go and find new territory. I started letting go the past and placing it with the good things in life. It is up to you to let good things flow in your mind and down to your heart. This is a great medicine for those who feel no one love or cares for them. You are born with love and it comes from you and flows from and up to the Father in heaven. Love is connecting your Heavenly Father to you. The past is the past and a person who keeps looking in the past will never be able to see clearly the road of the future. If you live, someone is going to try to still your inner beauty. Don't allow them to get in. Put a pop up blocker in front of you. When negative energy comes toward you flee! When it tries to attack you, pray! If it began to penetrate, rebuke! You have that authority through Jesus Christ. Never let anyone takeaway your inner beauty. God's grace covers every flaw, hurt or damages we can think or imagine. When I stop allowing others to hurt me then I could no longer be made fragile. God than impress the glory of beauty into my heart. My personality transformed, and I became an optimistic person when it came to the flaws. You must become real with yourself. You must ask yourself, is the problem you or me? Even though you have been hurt by love ones, you should remember, your healing starts on the inside.

Personality...

The second domain to self-awareness is *"Personality"* which means your character, traits, or behavior that is peculiar to you as an individual. Personality stems from your heart. Your personality causes you to be who you are. Paul admitted that he had personality problems when he addressed the church of Corinthians, yet, he did not let it get the best of him because of whom he trusted in.

³ And I was with you in weakness, and in fear, and in much trembling.

⁴ And my speech and my preaching was not with enticing words of man's wisdom, but in demonstration of the Spirit and of power." (I Corinthians 2: 3-4) KJV.

We were taught that our personalities come from our genetic make-up or DNA. But according to the word of God, we were created before we were in our mother's womb. You are not born with all your personally. Some of your specific personalities are cultivated by your surroundings. They are produced either by fleshly desires or spiritual desires. The molding starts from infant to five years old. We tend to ignore the personalities of infants and toddlers, but this is the foundation of personalities. Are you wondering why a two-year-old put a cup on a coaster when placing it on the table? It is a learn personality from the surroundings. The child will probably end up a perfectionist if the behavior continues to be modeled.

Some of your personal behaviors come from childhood; therefore, you should retrain yourself to think differently. It is up to you to allow either flesh or spirit to mold your personality. God's desire is for you to value the fruit of the Spirit (Galatians 5: 22-26), because this is the character and personality Jesus Christ portrayed when he walked the earth. God's desire is for you to become Christ-like. God values the fruit of the Spirit above our own intellectual personality, because this is the mind and personality of His origin.

I became frail in deceit…

I am reminded of what David said in Psalm 39: 4 [4] *LORD, make me to know mine end, and the measure of my days, what it is: that I may know how frail I am.,* (KJV)

David knew that only God could identify the problem that was going on with him. David was persevering through a trial, but didn't know the purpose. God was trying to get David to recognize he is weak without Him and all things exist through Him. Through this scripture, I began to realize that I had become weak and impressionable and needed the divine guidance of God.

Sometimes voids appear in your life, but you don't know what it is coming from. Until, recently, I found out most women whom father was abusive or absent in the home tend to leave a void in individuals lives. Also, women with missing fathers tends to go from relationship to relationship quickly than women who have a relationship with their father. To fill the void, they began to blame others and search for something or someone to make them happy (It didn't dawn on me this was the place God wanted his love to reside).

Hiding behind abuse and control, we tend to get even with past hurt and pain by becoming something that is not you, perhaps changing into a monster. Your revenge becomes showing the world you are "the best". You become competitive and everything you accomplish had to be at the top and determined to be excellent. Before you know it, excellence was driving you into a world of deceit. There is nothing wrong with excellence if the right person is driving. Sometimes excellence can land you in the wilderness. If I would have allowed God to drive excellence I would have landed in success, but because I was driving I had a strong desire to be successful in everything I did. It took God to show me how frail I was. God allowed my frailty to display when I continued to be driven by success, which is the third domain for self-awareness.

Success...

The third domain in self-esteem is *"success"*. Success is the achievement of something desired. God's view of success is totally the opposite of the world. You should never let success get to your head, because it will start feeding your heart. In the book of Philippians Paul counted all his accomplishments as nothing.

[7] But what things were gain to me, those I counted loss for Christ.

[8] Yea doubtless, and I count all things but loss for the excellency of the knowledge of Christ Jesus my Lord: for whom I have suffered the loss of all things, and do count them but dung, that I may win Christ,

[9] And be found in him, not having mine own righteousness, which is of the law, but that which is through the faith of Christ, the righteousness which is of God by faith: (Philippians 3: 7-9) KJV

Paul was reaching toward the goal of satisfaction when it came to gaining things in this world. His success was total dependency on God. Paul no longer saw himself as needing those things he counted loss, especially when he calls them "rubbish". Rubbish is something you discard because you don't need it anymore and the value of it becomes worthless. Sometimes rubbish is fertilizer for other things to grow. Paul's accomplishments in this world had become worthless, because his focus was no longer on this world's rewards. The rubbish in Paul's life was used to reprove and restore and prepare him for the task before him.

The rubbish in your life is the fertilizer to take you out of the remote position and drive you into the area where you will find hope, restoration and divine success. Success in this world can bring many rewards especially to women, but divine success brings about completeness, something that worldly success cannot compete with. When you become successful in this world, you *"feel"* You have become stronger, independent and desirable. But when you become divinely successful you *"are"* stronger, dependable, and desirable and all the voids in your life become sealed because of your relationship with God…then He becomes your Heavenly Father and not just "God".

Deceit plants a seed…

Lesson to learn. When someone loves you; it is difficult for them to hurt you and especially quickly hurt you. Your self-esteem and self-image will decline when you are trying to satisfy others and forget about yourself. Your personal appearance will have declined, and you will no longer cared about what you think or felt, because all the attention will be directed toward pleasing someone else. God is not an abuser and he did not create you to be abuse. If you are being abuse, get out in a hurry, because the damage starts small, but escalates into a mountain. You are too carefully, beautifully made to allow anything or anyone tear down your masterpiece.

I suffered for many years trying to find my identity, because I allowed someone else to take my identity and control it. There is nothing tangible in this world that can satisfy the hunger for acceptance, but God Almighty. If I wasn't focus on self I would have notice the walls God place to direct me. Now I look back and realize God was with me all the time giving me direction, but I fail to adhere to the traffic lights.

When you escape from captivity, you must go to a place of restoration. I needed some character building, because difficult situations and mishaps somehow was becoming a compass leading me into grasping tangible things to fill the void spots in my life. When I was in my early twenties, my marriage was about to be destroyed through Satan's tactics. This was one of the weakest points in my life. I needed a "Life Savior", not a "life saver"; not something to Band-Aid for a few stolen moments and then show up again.

In 1982, God sent me redemption through a family of faith. This family began to nurture me and help me to feel good about myself. But, I realize, I was going through the motions and had not turned my life over to God. I was only building my life on the circumstances around me and not realizing that circumstances do change. I needed to be taught "relationship" and not "having church"; therefore, the imperfection that was bestowed upon me was diminishing more and more. My focus was on getting to know God as a Father and not just "church".

Self-forgiveness...

The last domain is *"self-forgiveness"* which means to pardon ourselves from the faults and offenses we have done to ourselves. When you forgive yourself, you are not held accountable for past actions. Forgiving yourself can be very difficult, especially when you have been scarred by the very incident. Trying to forget something that hurt you can take a lifelong process without the help and guidance of God.

The problem with self-forgiveness is remembering it no more. God is not telling you that you will have amnesia. The Greek word for *"remember"* is *"mnaomai"* which means a fixture in the mind or being mindful. Therefore, God is saying to you He doesn't fix your sins in His mind anymore, but He didn't say there would be no consequences. Repentance leaves a non-revolving door; going out and never returning. Likewise, you must not fix in your mind past disappointments and failures. God has removed your faults; therefore, arm yourself with the same compassion.

Lack of self-forgiveness can cause you to be in bondage with yourself and someone else. Especially when they have forgiven you and you continue to act on your hurt from the situation. When you do this, you are giving that person the upper hand to control you like a puppet. Don't let anyone have the upper hand on your life, let go and let God strengthen your courage.

A healthy body can diminish through unforgiving. Being unforgiving can eat your insides as though a canker worm has attacked. The results deteriorate your self-esteem and transfers some of yours enter power to the one that you fail to forgive. Whether you know it or not; you are now being control internally by that person and sometimes externally when you allow your actions to be demonstrated. When you allow an unforgiving spirit to control your personality, you are denying the power of God in your life. His grace is sufficient for every flaw in your life. I had to realize that God is a God of a second chance...third chance and so on. God is a chance of chances. For He is God! But please don't try to use this as an excuse, because your chances may run out. We don't realize how much and idle mind can destroy, but I have learned from my trials and tribulations, God can deliver, restore and give you more than you deserve through His grace and mercy.

After suffering for many years, I could forgive myself and others. I believed if God wouldn't have allowed me to suffer and feel alienated, I wouldn't be spiritually anointed today. It was through the suffering, the clarity about me came forth. The hurt and disappoints were compasses guiding me to my true purpose of existence. It wasn't about me, but about the child that God chose to place In my mother's womb fifty-eight years ago, and for this I give Him the glory. I realized it was never about me. I was called from my mother's womb to be the evangelist, philanthropist, humanitarian, prophet, author and teacher that God has greatly revealed through His spirit.

My life learning: imperfection in a woman cannot be filled with tangible objects, because sooner or later you will become more fragile and need more filling to continue portraying the false image you have given yourself. It is imperative you realized the cries of desiring to be better are from the heart searching for the real you. The suffering you go through in learning whom you or can be not compared to the glory that is about to be revealed through what you are about to become. Through obedience to God you will learn who you are and not be a silhouette of who you think you are. When you step out of the shadow of life and walk into the presence of life you will press toward your goal; loving inside your inner woman and look forward to being Christ-like outside. Substitutes will no longer be an alternative and your inside assurance will reflect what you portray in life.

Chapter 4

It Doesn't Matter What "You" Think

When you give in to worthlessness, you deny the power of grace in our lives. Allowing the thoughts of others to dictate your future is a dangerous state of mind to be in. Being caught up in what people think of you can cause you to "lose yourself". Therefore, you must conquer this delusional feeling and move on to the perfection of our faith. Look in the mirror and realize people who control others don't have control themselves. We are in a world where the majority wants to be seen and hear, so why not, allow the thoughts of others control the way you think and act. If you do, you are becoming a robot and not a person. Most people don't even think about you at all. You have this guilt complex stimulating inside of you worrying about the other person's thoughts. It is a 24 hour plus job, dealing with the battles of your own. Sometimes you forget the things in which you battle with have already been conqueror through the blood of Jesus. Don't try to win a battle, but keep the battle in the winning mode; because God has already sent us a warrior (Jesus) and He conquered it all on the cross thousands of years ago, so why not be a cheerleader and say, "GO Jesus!" But because of fear we tend to go into the battle and get in the way which leads us to defeat.

I believe "fear" is the ultimate factor in defeat. When you walk in thinking "it is a losing battle", you might as well go in with no defense. Since you have already have given fear the upper hand. Fear of failure has always attacked individual's self-esteem. You must be aware of the author, which is "Satan". Fear does not come from God and He is not the author. God is the author and finisher of our faith not fears. I believe the center of fear is no more than you failing to test or walk into an area you are not familiar with. Fear always visits when there is doubt. Doubt comes from not knowing. We all have some type of doubt, but it is up to us how quickly it leaves. I always say, "It should leave you as quickly as a snap of the finger". Therefore, you want to be giving to much thought to "doubt". To put it in a nut shell it is all about the mindset.

"For God hath not given us the spirit of fear: but of power, and of love, and of a sound mind." (II Timothy 1:7) KJV

Every action starts with a thought and every thought starts with visually. With that note, let's start with the origin of everything…the mind. The mind dictates, and the body performs. I am reminded of an incident that happened a few years ago, I had an infirmity which causes me to have extremely anemia. I was asleep in my bed and when I awaken I could not get up to walk. What I didn't know, I had severely low blood. When I tried to stand up to walk, my brain signals could not connect in my mind to tell my legs to move. I knew scientifically this was a fact, but never experience it until then. This incident gave me validity on the brain controlling the emotions and actions of the body. Now I can relate to Paul addressing Timothy about God giving us a sound mind, because a sound mind demonstrates through our day to day actions and gives us the capability to trust God.

Sound Mind…

Is a sound mind essential? Yes, it is. The phrase *"sound mind"* in the Greek translation means, *to discipline or correct…teach to be sober…. self-control.* There are several scriptures in the bible which talks about *sound* and *sober.* These two words are synonyms, therefore when I talk about *sound;* I am also referring to *sober.* A sound mind is one that is clear, listens to God and is determining to please God. This type of mind is not easily distracted and gets all its clarity through the Holy Spirit. If you continue to live or entertain fear you are ineffectively trusting God. We must take our imperfections and lay them at the throne of God. He wants you to be aware of your imperfections, but realize He is the one who perfects everything. Knowing this, you can live a sound life with a sound mind. Fear will no longer take precedence over your faults, because you will have the victory through Jesus Christ, the author, and the one who completes your faith (your imperfections). Somehow, we have allowed people to complete our faith, instead of pressing toward the grace God has given us. We often beat up ourselves for things we don't have control over. Sound mind and sober mind is a spiritual personally, which causes an individual to be strong even when they are weak, because they adhere to the voice of God. A sound or sober mind does have grace and causes you to be less judgmental and more optimistic.

Be less the judge...

Sometimes your mind plays tricks on you when others are thinking about you. You tend to think the negative. Most of the time the person isn't thinking about you, but you think they are because you are accustoming to having negative thoughts about yourself. This type of behavior causes a person to be highly critical of themselves and others, which leads to a person being very defensive in most of their actions. Sometimes it will reflect in personal relationships and flow into your professional career habits, which can cause others to not want to deal with you. You very rarely hear a positive person defending themselves, because they have knowledge of who they are and knows God has their back. What better defense attorney!

The bible states:

3 For I say, through the grace given unto me, to every man that is among you, not to think of himself more highly than he ought to think; but to think soberly, according as God hath dealt to every man the measure of faith. (Romans 12:3) KJV

Look at the phrase *"more highly"* in the above passage. When you think of the word "more" you are looking at something that is beyond the norm or ability. Our excellence is through God not ourselves, so you don't think excellence; you walk into the grace of excellence. When you walk into the grace of excellence you nail all your imperfections to the cross and the blood of Jesus makes you perfect. Therefore, you have no need to boast on your looks, skills or tangible things you have.

Paul was saying to the Roman Church to not put your thoughts beyond your capability, because whatever you cannot do God's *"grace"* is sufficient.

You are not superwoman, but God is!

Being realistic about thoughts…

Our thoughts are a control mechanism for the heart. Therefore, it is imperative to have a sound mind.

You are wondering why no one wants to be around you. Maybe you need to check out the words you say. This happens often with a person who has low self-esteem. Remember, everyone is not going to agree with everything you say, but if you give them time they will consider it. We need to be kinder to ourselves through our thoughts, and then we would spend less time thinking others are talking negative about us.

The mind feeds the heart and the heart is the control panel for our emotions. When a mind has a lot of hurt and pain it is accustoming to speaking pain. Eventually, you will drive people away and it will be difficult to build new relationships. I am reminded of a woman I knew who had a lot of mishaps in her life from childhood to adulthood. She had been abused as a child, sour marriage, and never received psychological nor spiritual counseling. Therefore, it spilled over into her personal relationships. She couldn't get along with anyone and she was always bitter. She thought sharing the experience with me would help, and it did, but she began sharing it with lots of people, until the pain became normal. But, she was delusional and fooling herself, because now it has become a monumental moment in her life, which she thought was okay. She had no peace and began to dwell on the pain, instead of the peace and joy God has provided for her. The pain this woman was feeling was also giving off a signal to other women that it was okay to feel this way. Don't you know your actions can offend others, especially when you are a believer of Christ? A mind that is concern with its own personal pain usually refuses healing and it spills over into others. It's okay to be realistic about thoughts, but don't let the painful ones control your entire life.

Chapter 5

Dealing with Negative Inner and Outer Circles

Run! Susie! Run! This is the creative punch line in the award-winning movie These words have become popular with many, but do we really know why that person was running and who She was running from. I am using Susie to relate to the female. Susie had two things against her, her adversary and her adversity; peers and braces on her legs. Susie didn't just walk out of this; Susie ran out of this. Susie met a friend name "Johnny" (inner circle), who cared about her so much until he was the very one to open the gateway for her to look beyond barriers she had in life. When Susie was walking, she was only a distance from her adversary, but when she started running, her peers were a distance and the very thing (the braces) which kept her from running became her savior. From this day forward, she didn't allow anything or anyone to stop her from moving forward. Even though she had learning disabilities, Susie used those abilities to take her into a world of success. The key hear was acceptance. Accepting who you are and changing only the things you have the power to change and leave the rest up to God. Acceptance is one area of life which dominates our decision making. So, what do you do? You allow anything and everything to guide you into a world of deceit and pain. It is up to the individual who they desire to reside in their circle; depending on who you chose the results can end up being devastating, especially if we choose pessimistic people. We are in a community of people who are desperate for attention and desperate to control someone else's life because they have lost control of their own.

We all know the story of Solomon and how God released and overflow of blessing to him. Solomon was one of the riches in the world, but he was negligent with his personal circle which causes him some repercussions. Later, Solomon wrote in Proverbs:

"Keep thy heart with all diligence; for out of It are the issues of life," (Proverbs 4.23) KJV

In other words, Solomon was instructing us to guard our hearts above everything, for in doing this we determine the direction of our life. Whatever is in the heart will come out. But who feeds the heart? We do. How do we feed the heart? Your thoughts feed the mind and then release an appetite for the heart to dictates to your surrounding circles.

Guard Your Heart…

Our rib cage is the protective organ of the heart. The same way the rib protects the heart, your mind and thoughts protect your heart. Whatever you feed the mind can either hurt or heal the heart. In the bible, you notice the heart is so delicate until, God gives us warnings about it. Out of the heart flows the issue of life. Your heart also determines your destiny. For instance, if you have decided to do something evil or good this comes out of the heart. Be aware of what you allow to come into your heart. Your circle influences the decisions of your heart. One example is, when you sit around people who think negative, their actions are to make themselves more appealing, this behavior can flow into your personal space and you began to feel this is an appropriate behavior. When you guard your heart, you are protecting your personality from allowing anything or anyone hurt you. Your heart is your physical and spiritual person. Therefore, it is vital you protect it physically and more so mentally. The heart is the physical organ and spiritual organism which define us as a living being. Therefore, you are living and not just existing. Happiness and sadness is orchestrated out of the heart. You have the right to decide who shares your heart. When a woman meets the opposite sex, her heart is automatically looking for a mate, this is in her genetic make-up. Deciding who will be the mate is up to which circle she pulls that relationship out of. The inner circle is who she allows to come into her personal space. The outer circle is vice versa.

We tend to look for relationships in our outer circle, because the heart likes challenges. When we go into our inner circle for relationships, we must be very observant and not move to fast, because this is where the sheep in wolves clothing is waiting. Many women have met Mr. Right in the wrong place and wrong time. You will know whether the person you chose to be in your inner circle is the right person for your mate. One thing for sure, he will accept you the way you are and, will be an asset not a liability. He will not destroy your positive self-esteem, if anything, he will compliment it. If you were once a happy person, and suddenly you see yourself sad or discontent, you probably chose the wrong person to be in your inner circle. This type of person you don't want to have a personal relationship with and keep them at a distance in your outer circle. The scriptures even tell us light and darkness doesn't mix.

[14] Be ye not unequally yoked together with unbelievers: for what fellowship hath righteousness with unrighteousness? and what communion hath light with darkness? (II Corinthians 6:14) KJV.

Light is the optimistic and darkness is the pessimistic. Even when you look at those words you can see the negative sound like a pest! Why are you allowing negative energy to come into your circle? Don't you know you can't commune with negative people? They will never understand your end of the spectrum. Disagreements will constantly arise between you and them; therefore, you will never be able to come to a consensus on anything. Henceforth, they will become more a harassment than a friend. It is so strange for a person in light to desire to be in dark, but it does happen. Darkness attracts them because they never been in the true light. You were just feeling some of the rays from a light bulb, which turn on and off. God's light never turns off. When you receive the true light in your life, darkness becomes your enemy; therefore, you walk into darkness beaming brightly until darkness can no longer linger, it must flee.

I can remember a young lady who had a cruel father and was looking for a way out, so she decided to leave home. She wanted a way out. Her father was cruel to her and her siblings. She wanted someone to love her and give love in return. Her search was through a male relationship. This woman really wanted love from her father, but she settled with love from a male relationship. She allowed this person to come into her inner circle, he destroyed her self-esteem. He abused her physically and mentally. Her desire to become successful had dwindled into a bottle full of tears. Pleasing herself was obsolete, but doing what he wanted was a priority. She found herself doing things she could only imagine and the words *"I will never do this"* came to life. The smile she once had, had turned upside down. She had lost the desire to be love and couldn't give love in return. All of this happened because she allowed a sheep in wolves clothing steal her heart. The only way she could overcome this was through the word of God. No matter how many times you drip away from God, He tends to be standing there waiting on you to rekindle the words He once spoken to you.

Instead of looking around for the answer, it was in front of her, but moreover, it was still in her heart, but the forces of evil had hidden it. Obedience to the word of God is the key to becoming beautiful and positive. She took her heart back, by loving God with all her heart, soul and mind and releasing herself from that controlling person. The beauty began to slowly reveal itself like water on a bounty paper towel. She no longer needed the love and acceptance from another man, but from God and He accepted her just the way she was. She even told me, "God doesn't control my actions. He prefers when I do things willingly for Him". I like that about Him". If you continue to hang around fire eventually you will be burned. Never test waters unless you are willing to swim in it, because it only takes a test for you to be convinced you can do it.

It is very important for women to be careful with their inner and outer circles. Only allow the positive in it. If you want your life to be fruitful and successful keep the inner circle limited with uplifting trustworthy relationships. If you want your heart to be filled with love from the opposite sex, wait on God to give and send you an ordained soul mate… this is another story. It is okay to go into either circle, but make sure you are being led by God and not your flesh, because negative inner or outer circle relationships can hurt and be very painful when you become vulnerable to them.

You have heard the saying, "birds of a feather flock together". Whether you believe it or not, this statement is true. How many different species of birds have you seen flying together…none? This is because they have a unified way of identifying themselves. Just like women have a unified way of identifying themselves. Most of the time this identification comes through our surrounding circle of acquaintances. I am not talking about people you occasionally know. I am talking about people you hang around daily and share your most intimate thoughts with. In this circle, you share your heart. You feel very comfortable with them. This can be dangerous, if you have negative energy inside it. You can be the most optimistic person, but if you continue to commune with pessimistic people, your positivity will become contaminated and before you will know it, your heart will become contaminated. The very thing you thought was *not* okay will become dominate, in other words "the norm". Methodically, a negative and a positive equal a negative. Therefore, you must stay away from negative people. Don't add or takeaway anything from them because whatever you accrue from them adds on to your energy and preferably starts deleting the positive. If you have a negative attitude, this only builds up more stuff you must get rid of. After you have built up this negative energy, it no longer becomes and energy, but a driving force. You can't allow anything or anybody to take part in you becoming the person God wants you to be.

Negative forces...

Today, negativity is on a rampage especially in women's hearts. Some have been through, sexual abuse, sexual assault, domestic violence, drug abuse and so on. This list keeps getting longer and longer. As the list goes on and on, negative energy changes into negative forces.

These forces are coming from the negative acts in this world and demonstrating themselves through the lives of women who once had high self-esteem. What do you do about these force...You must drive them out and take back your physical and mental state. This force can only be driven out through the blood of Jesus, which is applied to your life immediately when you received salvation. I am not talking about church going or joining a church. I am literally talking about soul saving sanctified salvation.

If someone steals something from you the normal reaction is to find a way of getting it back. I can recall a message which was preached to me years ago, "Go and get what the devil stole from you". The devil didn't steal your negative attributes, because he is the owner of negativity. What he does steal is your integrity and dignity through taking away the positive characteristics you have nurtured so many years. He tries to put your positive energy into captivity. In I Samuel, chapter 30, David was confronted with losing all his possessions and they were carried away by the enemy. David didn't just go after it immediately; he seeked the Lord for guidance;

".⁸ *And David enquired at the* LORD, *saying, Shall I pursue after this troop? shall I overtake them? And he answered him, Pursue: for thou shalt surely overtake them, and without fail recover all.*" (I Samuel 30:8) KJV

As I read this chapter repeatedly, I realized David knew it was up to God what he possessed and, he knew if God told him not to pursue, God can provide and give him more than what he lost. These were not just worldly possessions he lost, but also his integrity. David was a king and he had statues and morals to adhere to. Same as, you as a woman have statues and morals to adhere to, therefore, you need to go and get back your positive personally and get it back now! The adversary can't use your positive personally…he can't. Therefore, he destroys it. Whatever you lost you rebuild through God, because it is only lost not deleted.

Deal with it…

Sometimes you want to take the things that are bothering you and lay them on the table. Even though your inside is willing the outside just should do it his or her way. It is so sad how your inside must dance to the performances on the outside. For instance, you may be portraying yourself as the humblest wife, but your inside is smothered with lies and deceit. You don't want others to see the real deal, so you pretend to be submissive toward your spouse. Furthermore, you gather all your ammo and decide to kill the enemy before it destroys you; instead you ended up bowing down just to save face. How hypocritical you can be when you are trying to be the epiphany of perfection. Perfection does not denote any mistakes, but how we deal with mistakes. God's grace is the closes we are going to get to perfection. The more you try to do well, the more you realize how mess up you are. Some even use the excuse, *"I am only playing the hand I was dealt"*. But the hand is not the problem, the player is. The player must know how to handle the hand to stay in the game, even so as much, becomes a winner. I say, "Use this same hand and play your cards to the best of your ability". Only hypocrites use excuses.

There is no excuse for failure, especially when you have the power to make a change. Even the noblest gambler knows how to take a losing hand and use it to stay in the game. Take back your perfections through Grace and grab a hold of it. Don't give up until you have reached the point of delivering the positive flow of life through it. God wants the least, because in having the least you can reach to the greatest and build a winning life.

There is nothing in this life you can't handle without the help of Our Heavenly Father. God sometimes distribute us with a taste of something small, so we can acquire a taste to develop something large. If you deal with your flaws, this will open the gateway for God to build you up on the inside to becoming an epiphany of greatest on the outside. There isn't anything in this world broken and don't need fixing. Yeah, you may see some glue, or tape here or there, but without the glue or tape, you will never be able to hold yourself. Items with glue or tape can be used but not without a force of help. The metaphors of glue and tape are only reminders of how fragile we are, and we need someone higher than us to hold us together.

Release the Negative person who hurt you!

It is vital for your health and for your spiritual healing to release positive energy daily into the negative arrows. Don't keep reminding yourself of the pain and hurt. If you need to get professional help, do so. If you need to get spiritual counseling, do so. I really didn't move forward until I started talking to counselors, pastors and spiritual advisors. Talk to confidential people. I realized I needed to pray for the person who hurt me and pray for God to heal them also. I prayed to God to let them see themselves and to allow them to become a better person. I had become more concern about the person, more so, than what they had done to me, because deep inside I really loved them. When you belong to Christ, hate is something difficult to do, no better how much you hurt.

Chapter 6

Place It on the Table

Since life is not about us alone, we must place ourselves in a distinguish category. Since sexual, mental, and physical abuse is predominantly toward the female. We must be ready with ammo to conquer the spirit of low self-esteem. Instead of guarding your affections, why not guard confidence. In doing so, we have put up iron bars as a defense mechanism. The bars are only up to keep the other person from getting to close, which gives you the opportunity to decide who resides or can come in and out of our territory. Looking back on my life, and the baby boomers, many of those children who are now in their late 40's are older has face many challenges in life because society didn't have the many protective laws in which they have now for individuals. Therefore, we are feeling the effect of the negativity through the behaviors of those individuals as adults. Some of them are sexual predators, mental and sexual abusers, behaviors problems and the list go on and on and as this continues it continues to nurture in our future children DNA's.

We must lay this stuff on the table... as women we should start protecting our future as individuals and our future seeds. We don't have to accept anything negative in front of us and if it is a diamond in the dust, let's take it, cultivate it and identity the true value. Just because it is covered in dirt doesn't mean it loses its value. *A diamond in dirt is still a diamond.* Most of the time when something has been covered so long it devalues itself. Perfect example, I knew a young lady who had a degree in fashion design. She could design beautiful dresses and sew them very well, but she remained in the southern area, so long, until when someone did discover her worth she was afraid to move forward. By the way she wanted to move forward but she was afraid of failure. You will never know what's out there unless you try. Failure is always a step-in success. When a baby walk, he or she always falls once or twice before that initial step...we can learn a lot from a baby. Somewhere inside of us there is something we always wanted to do but we allowed others to devalue us or we devalued ourselves. Know your worth. Quit looking around at others and comparing your worth to other folks. You should have a snap shot already of what your portfolio is in your head and have a pretty picture of what you are worth in a relationship as a woman and professionally in a career. You shouldn't have to go on the internet to look up professionally what you are worth. Professionally, always keep your chin up even when you are rejected from a promotion. My son once told me these words *"Man's rejection is God's protection"* in a sense, this is true. Everything that look good, may not be good for you. Also, it does not take away from your slice of value. Sometimes God allow us to go through the motions to let us know we are still valuable, but He has something picked out specifically just for us. Also, God knows what is ahead.

God's children don't' chase promotions, we walk into our purpose". It is so important we remember this when we are rejected in our professional life. Some of us will probably never have degrees, but we can share our wisdom, knowledge and life experiences which gives out life dividends and returns even when we no longer exist in this present world. This stuff is Priceless!

Single or Divorced and lonely... Most single women remain single because they tend to go into a relationship looking for a husband. Wrong Answer! Go into a relationship not looking for anything in return. Just be friends. Friends is the best relationships and make the best breakups! Why because .... friends can move on without having any issues.... Please don't look for a man to make you complete. Your completeness is in God. The more you seek God, the more He knows when you need a mate. The more you go looking for a mate, the more Satan will send you his mate. In the scripture, Adam was tending to the things of God and God saw Adam needed a mate...Adam didn't even know He needed one (Genesis 2:18). God Knows when to bring in the other half.

Married and Lonely... Married women do get lonely sometime, especially when you been in the relationship a long time and your mate take you for granite. The other half probably think you not going anywhere and you probably feel like you are now a piece of wall paper in the house. Well…it's time for you to get notice. Remember 10 – 20 years ago, the person who use to be happy, smiling. If there is any beauty left inside of them only God Himself can see it. It is so important you awaken and smell the aroma of beauty. Married couples need to have dates more often to rekindle the fire again. I am not talking about a movie. I am talking about real table cloth restaurant dinner and if you have small children pay a babysitter…get the fire started again in the marriage. Most Christian divorces are because we don't balance our life styles. Jesus wants us to balance this thing. He instituted the family before the church. If we break up the family what will happen to the church! Let's get it together people! Go back to Adam and Eve, they had in on in the Garden! It is so sad when the world system knows how to keep a woman or man happy and we still trying to learn how to date. When God wrote the book, and instituted it! Be the woman God called you to be!

Quit hiding behind the mirror and be the reflection of confidence. Only you can tear down your walls and it take you to build them back up.

PEARLS Cultivated by the Master… Since the beginning women has been responsible for messing up things. Eve in the Garden of Eden. But you know what, God didn't charge Eve, He charge Adam, and the cycle is still going on today, man is still blaming the women for the behavior of the children in our society, but the victim is still the women. Women are like pearls we go through a lot to be a woman. Pearls go through a lot to become a pearl. Peals cost you something and it gives you value. It cost us something to be women, but we have value. The more a woman values herself, the more she will be valued. It doesn't matter what others think. Her children's, children will call her blessed and they will be blessed. Her seed will carry on her wisdom and knowledge through her DNA. Pearls have a luster that must be guarded and can't be cleaned with anything. Likewise, women are an attractive valuable commodity to the opposite sex which is valuable, and no one can take this away.

Therefore, let's take the inside that has been literally raped and rebuild it, so we can be that beautifully wonderfully made creature God intended for us to be. The outside is just a mirror reflection of the activity going on inside. Turn that thing inside out and grasp the real woman who is more precious than diamonds and more beautiful than any precious stone and has beauty that shines before she even appears.

Thing to Remember....

***If you see yourself or reflection of some else in this book please don't hesitate to seek Professional or Spiritual-Christian counseling for that individual.**

Daily Mirror Quote:

In the Mirror

"Mirror, Mirror on My Wall,
this Is the Only One you going to get from this wall…
I Love this beauty, it cannot Fall,
because It was created by the Greatest of All"
(Then Blow a kiss at yourself).
Say:
"See you tomorrow!"

An Instrument Broken and tested depends on
"The Master" for strength to be used again.
This is when perfection begins to reveal itself

. Resa Farnell

Printed in the United States
By Bookmasters